EAST ANGLIAN
BRANCH LINE ALBUM

The 2-4-0 type of locomotive had evolved very early in railway history and for years had been the mainstay of the running department.

The last examples of the type to survive in this country were the old Great Eastern Railway Class E4s and in September 1957 there were only four left in service.

It was still possible at that time to see two members of the class side by side at Long Melford and this photo shows Class E4 2-4-0 No. 62785 entering on a Cambridge-Colchester train, while at the other platform Class E4 2-4-0 No. 62797 is waiting to make the connection before leaving for Bury St. Edmunds.

On withdrawal in December 1959, No. 62785 was restored at Stratford works to its original condition and is now preserved at the Railway Museum, York.

EAST ANGLIAN BRANCH LINE ALBUM

by Dr. Ian Cameron Allen

Oxford Publishing Co. Oxford

In June 1934 Class J15 0-6-0 L.N.E.R. No. 7911 negotiates the short branch to Haverhill South, near Colne Valley Junction.
The line from Colne Valley Junction running down to join the former Great Eastern Railway line at Haverhill North can be seen to the right of the old house shown next to the locomotive.

Negatives and platemaking
Oxford Litho Plates

Printed by Blackwell's
in the City of Oxford

Published by
Oxford Publishing Co.
8 The Roundway,
Headington, Oxford.

INTRODUCTION

To Bill Harvey, a great East Anglian railwayman

I first began to explore the East Anglian railway system over fifty years ago. The country branches in particular completely fascinated me.

Ten years later I came to live and work in rural Suffolk, at the end of a short branch line. Part of my practice was in an area served by the Mid Suffolk Light Railway (by now absorbed into the L.N.E.R.). I thus heard from my patients of the branch line heyday, and also, from some of the older ones, of the days before they had a railway at all.

I can thus understand, probably better than most, the spirit of enterprise which lay behind the building of a local railway, and what it meant to the local population.

What may be considered the first main line railway was opened in 1829 between Liverpool and Manchester and was primarily for the carriage of freight. Its promoters were surprised at the demand for passenger travel. Its success was so great that within the next thirty years the basic framework of today's British Rail Inter-City network was already completed. Every town and village wanted to be on the railway and hundreds of lines were promoted, with enthusiasm, but no financial acumen.

The Railway Mania burst in 1848 when a lot of money was lost. The small lines that were built soon amalgamated and on 7th August 1862 The Great Eastern Railway Company was incorporated, which included nearly all the railways in East Anglia.

No better title, reflecting the spirit of the age so well, could have been chosen. The Great Eastern Railway served a relatively sparsely populated agricultural area with a basic seasonal freight traffic. It never became one of the rich railway companies, but it was led by men whose vision and enterprise have had a lasting effect.

There are few short lines in East Anglia. The absence of hills and valleys meant that there were very few places where geographical obstacles cut short the progress of lines.

The main line system developed into two lines: The first was from London to Norwich and Yarmouth and the second from London to Cambridge and Kings Lynn. These were connected by long cross-country branches which built up into a co-ordinated whole.

In this book I have tried to show pictorially this system of minor East Anglia lines which, in the great days of the Railway, were regarded as feeders to the main lines, but which, as road competition developed, came to be considered as suckers and as such had to be cut out.

The Railways reached their zenith in the days before the 1914-18 war. Road competition developed very quickly in the nineteen-twenties and by 1938 the railways launched a campaign for a fair deal. Then followed the 1939-45 war when the branch lines reached their finest hour. The full story of their achievement throughout this period has never been told.

With the return of peace it was clear that many of the branch lines were redundant, and Dr. Beeching will always be associated with their closure. As a countryman I always regret that his brief from the Government was only destructive, and feel that a great opportunity to co-ordinate rail and road transport was missed.

I am indebted to Mr. R. S. Joby for information about the East curve at Reedham junction. His book "Forgotten Railways — East Anglia" gives a full account of all the lines illustrated in this book. I am also indebted to Mr. John Watling and Mr. Keith Garwood for information about the Mistley Tramway.

I would like also to thank Mrs T. G. Hovenden for her help in preparing this book.

Ian Cameron Allen

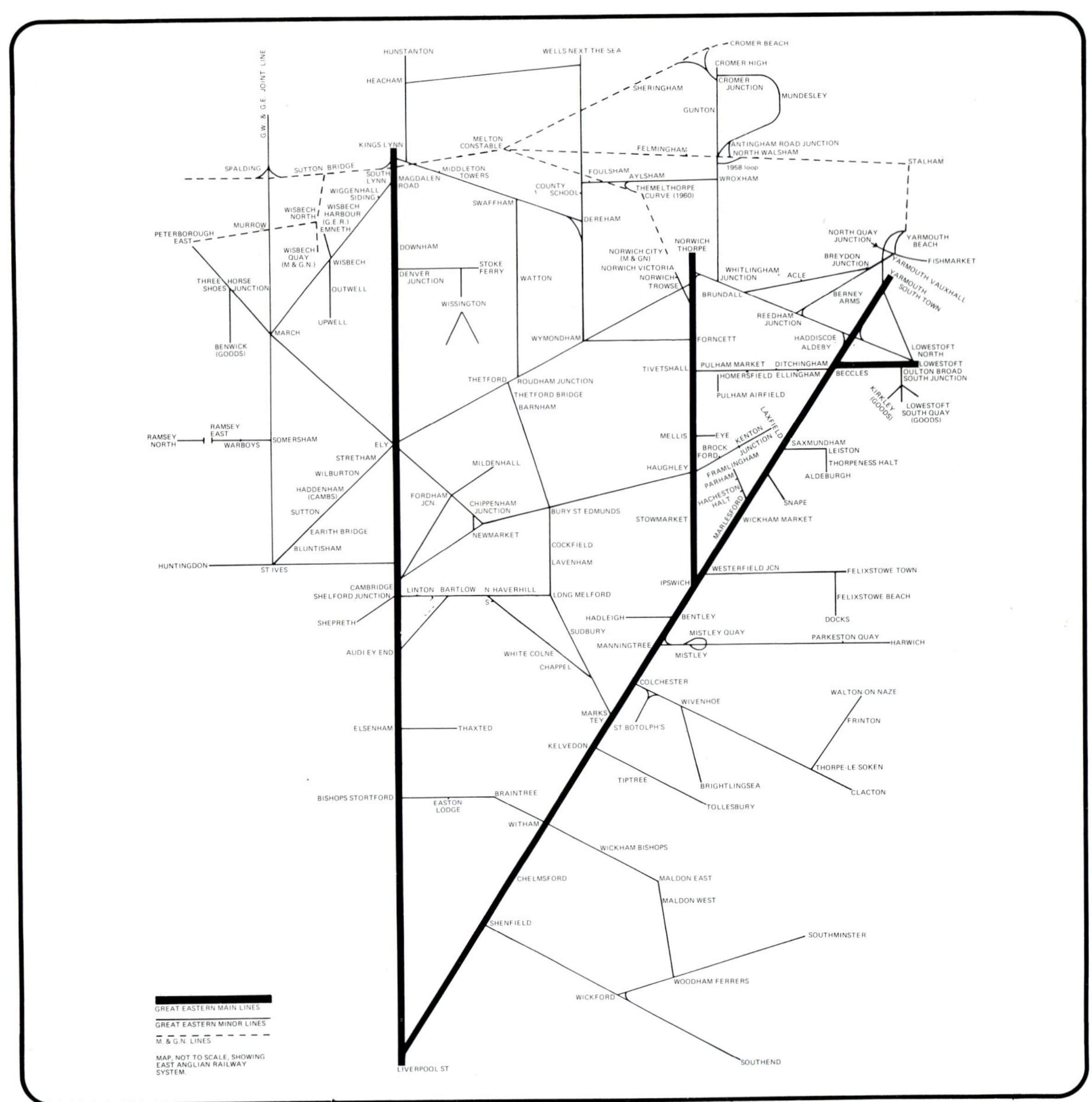

Fig. 1 At Chelmsford, in 1957, a fast freight train, hauled by the unique Class K5 2 cylinder rebuilt 2-6-0 ▶ No. 61863, is passing a stock train which is waiting in the loop, hauled by Class B17/6 4-6-0 No. 61605 *"Lincolnshire Regiment"*.

The freight train is composed of the traditional short wheel base four-wheeled trucks. Many of them would have originated on a country branch line and would have been taken to the junction station to be picked up by the express freight train.

The stock train, as it was always called in East Anglia, conveyed urgent perishable traffic of every description, much of which had also originated on various country branch lines.

In earlier days it had conveyed horse boxes and vans full of milk churns. More recently the milk had been conveyed in bulk in tank trucks.

By the end of the nineteen-fifties most of this lucrative traffic had been lost to the road and the branches could no longer pay their way. Soon most of them were to disappear completely and the fast freight trains to be replaced by Freightliners and by trains conveying bulk loads. Both these services run direct from one centre to another.

Fig. 2 Because of the superiority of railways for the conveyance of heavy traffic such as coal, sand or sugar ▶ beet, many of the rural branches survived for the transport of freight about ten years after they had been closed to passenger traffic.

Class J68 0-6-0T No. 68666 on a freight train is passing Wickham Bishops on the branch line from Witham to Maldon.

This branch retained its passenger service till 7th September 1964 — longer than most owing to its proximity to London. Freight traffic ceased on 18th April 1966.

▲ *Fig. 3* The branch to Maldon was opened from Witham in 1848. In 1861 the population of Maldon was 4,785, and it was always regarded by the Great Eastern Railway as an important town.

Here, in April 1931, is the Maldon branch train at Witham. The locomotive is Class F7 2-4-2T L.N.E.R. No. 8310. The train of two six-wheeled coaches and a six-wheeled van, chiefly for the conveyance of milk churns, was the typical small country branch formation at this time.

The locomotive was built in 1910, being one of a class of twelve designed for light branch duties. In practice they proved too small to cope with fluctuating traffic demands. No. 8310 was transferred to Scotland in September 1931.

▲ *Fig. 5* Maldon was also served by a branch from Woodham Ferrers, on the Southminster branch, which was opened in 1889.

Class F4 0-4-4T L.N.E.R. No. 8109 is entering Woodham Ferrers with the Maldon train in April 1931.

The passenger service was withdrawn on 10th September 1939 and the freight service on 1st April 1953 (though the short section from Maldon East to Maldon West remained open till 1st January 1959).

▼ *Fig. 6* This is the Maldon branch train leaving Witham in April 1957, when, owing to the failure of the usual Class F5 2-4-2T locomotive, it was being hauled by Class J69/1 0-6-0T No. 68579.

To the right of the picture can be seen the track bed of the loop which was used on summer Saturdays between 1890 and 1895 by a through train from Southend to Colchester. By using loops at Wickford and Maldon, through running was possible, though after a couple of years reversal was made at Maldon (East).

About this time the threat of a German invasion of England on the East coast began to emerge. One wonders if any military considerations of the defence of London were taken into account when planning this branch. The normal traffic potential from Southend to Colchester could never have justified such a service.

Fig. 4 The Witham-Maldon branch train is approaching Wickham Bishops station behind Class F5 2-4-2T No. 67189 in the final days of steam working.

The station had no signals but a lamp was provided on a post to indicate its whereabouts to the driver at night.

Because of some weak trestle bridges, the Class F5 were the heaviest locomotives allowed over the branch.

A through train from Liverpool Street to Maldon on Saturday afternoons had to be hauled by a Class J15 0-6-0.

Fig. 8 A Light Railway Act became law in 1896 which allowed branch lines to be built to a lower standard than was demanded for main lines. Speed, however, had to be severely limited as a consequence of this lower standard. (The same year saw the repeal of the Act which required any mechanical vehicle on the road to be preceded by a man carrying a red flag. Though nobody realised it at the time, the repeal of this Act was the beginning of the end of the branch line age).

One light railway to be built under the 1896 Act was the branch from Kelvedon to Tollesbury, the first section of which was opened in 1904 and which was completed to Tollesbury Pier in 1907.

This photo, taken in June 1936, shows Class J67/1 0-6-0T L.N.E.R. No. 7161 which has just arrived at Kelvedon Low Level station with a mixed train of passenger and freight vehicles. Provided one was not in a hurry, there was no better way to see the country than in one of these trains. At every station there would be a leisurely stop, when sometimes one would be shunted in and out of the sidings and between stations the trucks would bang and clatter behind the passenger vehicles.

▲ *Fig. 7* Class F5 2-4-2T No. 67192 is leaving Witham for Braintree. At the time of writing this section is being electrified and thus will become part of the suburban network.

From Braintree the branch ran on to Bishop's Stortford. Passenger services on this section were withdrawn on 3rd March 1952. Traffic to the sugar beet factory at Felsted finally ceased on 1st April 1969.

During the blitz on London in the 1939-45 war, this branch was sometimes used by Ipswich trains when the main line was blocked. One of the branch stations, Easton Lodge, was built in the early eighteen-nineties by the Countess of Warwick, at her own expense. This was for the convenience of H.R.H. The Prince of Wales, who was a frequent visitor by the Royal Train.

Fig. 9 This picture also taken in 1936, shows an occasion when ▶ the Kelvedon-Tollesbury train was composed of four coaches. The two six-wheeled 3rd class brakes had been converted from standard stock. The seating was of the tramway type, so that tickets could be issued by the guard. The coaches were set very low off the ground so that orthodox platforms could be dispensed with.

The two bogies had been built in 1884 for the Wisbech and Upwell Tramway and had been transferred to Kelvedon when the Tramway was closed to passenger traffic on 2nd January 1928.

The second vehicle from the locomotive is a most interesting four-wheeled van. No standard Great Eastern Railway branch train formation was ever completed without a van, chiefly for the conveyance of milk churns.

The locomotive is class J67/1 0-6-0T L.N.E.R. No. 7161.

Fig. 11 From Marks Tey a long cross-country branch ran to Cambridge. The branch platform, still used by the Sudbury trains, is single track. So till the beginning of the 1939-45 war, a Colchester-Cambridge train had to run into the up main line platform, reverse across the down main line into the down loop, and then move forward onto the branch.

In October 1931, Class F3 2-4-2T L.N.E.R. No. 8042 is shown on a Colchester-Cambridge train moving on to the branch. The operation was supervised by the Station Master and Foreman.

The working from Sudbury was traditional. Early morning trains left there for both Cambridge and Colchester. The locomotives then worked a round trip over the branch and returned to Sudbury in the evening. Next morning the locomotive, which had come in from Cambridge, continued on to Colchester and vice versa, thus working a 48 hour cycle.

▲ *Fig. 12* The Eastern Counties Railway reached Colchester North from Shoreditch in 1843, and in 1846 the Eastern Union Railway continued the line to Ipswich. In 1849 the Colchester, Stour Valley, Sudbury and Halstead Railway opened a line from Colchester North to Colchester-Hythe. In 1863 the Tendring Hundred Railway continued the line from Colchester-Hythe to Wivenhoe and then reached Brightlingsea in 1866 and Walton-on-the-Naze in 1867.

In 1866 the Tendring Hundred Railway opened a new station in Colchester, called St. Botolphs. This was nearer the town than the North station and was also designed to serve the military camp then under construction. It was at the apex of a triangle so that trains could either run direct to Wivenhoe or else take one side of the triangle into St. Botolphs, where they would reverse and continue to Wivenhoe on the other side.

In the nineteen-fifties Colchester St. Botolphs was still a very rural station, as this photo shows. Class B17/6 3 cylinder 4-6-0 No. 61666 *"Nottingham Forest"* is approaching on a Colchester North-Clacton local train. The Brightlingsea branch train is in the siding.

Fig. 14 Class J15 0-6-0 No. 65468 running round its train at Brightlingsea.

In its heyday this branch, like so many other seaside branches, carried a considerable fish traffic. Hence the name "Crab and Winkle" became a general term of endearment for the local train, and was used as such at Brightlingsea.

▲ *Fig. 15* In the census of 1861 the population of Walton-on-the-Naze was 697; that of Frinton (which consisted of six houses) was 29; and of Great Clacton 1,280. It is curious that the Tendring Hundred Railway built their line to Walton-on-the-Naze in 1866, but did not build the branch to Clacton from Thorpe-le-Soken until 1882.

In spite of the development of the area which followed the opening of the railway, Clacton remained a typical branch line till the rebuilding of the station in 1929, when the short original turntable was replaced, and Class B12 and B17 4-6-0's could be employed on the residential trains. Hitherto the largest locomotives allowed had been the Super Claud 4-4-0s.

The line to Clacton from Thorpe-le-Soken was doubled in 1941. The branch was electrified in 1959 as far as Colchester, and in 1962 express electric trains began running through to Liverpool Street, when it may be said to have become a main line.

In this photo, taken in March 1959, Class N7/4 0-6-2T No. 69612 is leaving Thorpe-le-Soken on a Colchester-Clacton local train, a few days before the experimental electric working of trains between Colchester and Clacton was inaugurated.

▲ *Fig. 16* Class N7/3 0-6-2T No. 69732 takes a rest between duties at Walton-on-the-Naze.

▼ *Fig. 17* In 1846, a few days after the opening of the railway, a very well patronised excursion was run to Rotterdam from stations between London and Ipswich, the ship sailing from Ipswich.

In 1854 the branch to Harwich was opened from Manningtree and travel to the Continent by this route quickly grew. In 1882 the Continental traffic had become too great for Harwich to handle and a new port was opened called Parkeston Quay. This was named after Mr. Parkes, the chairman of the Great Eastern Railway at that time, and Mr. Stone, the engineer responsible for its construction.

This photo, taken in June 1936, shows a remarkable Great Eastern Railway survival. Class J65 0-6-0T L.N.E.R. No. 7254, still with its original low cab roof, is running into Parkeston Quay on a workman's train from Harwich. The train is comprised of old Great Eastern Railway six-wheelers.

A frequent service used to be run for the benefit of men working at the Dock. Even today there are still one or two such trains.

▲ *Fig. 18* The Harwich-Parkeston Quay workman's train at Harwich in 1960. The locomotive is Class N7/3 0-6-2T No. 69691.

To the left, Class J19 0-6-0 No. 64643 is waiting for the arrival of the Zeebrugge-Harwich train ferry. This was opened in 1924. At high or low tide there could be a very stiff gradient either up or down to the deck of the ferry, requiring a powerful locomotive to carry out the necessary shunting.

▼*Fig. 19* At Mistley, the first station on the Harwich branch, a tramway ran down to the Quay. This left the up sidings, where the cutting can still be seen, and curled round under the main line, through a bridge which survived till 1947.

Traffic over the tramway was worked by horses. In 1898 they were handling over three thousand wagons a year. Authorisation was therefore given for the construction of a very steep incline on the down side which is still in use. To reach the quay, trains which were locomotive hauled, had to reverse where the new incline joined the old tramway.

For several years the only traffic has been to a granary, but recently there has been an increase in cargoes handled on the quay.

In this photo, taken in the final days of steam, Class J19 0-6-0 No. 64652 is shown toiling up the incline with a light load of two trucks.

3559
L N E R

65459

Fig. 20 In 1885 a through service from Harwich to Doncaster was instituted (later extended to York and with through coaches to Manchester and Liverpool). This took an avoiding loop at Manningtree. Some of the Ipswich-Harwich local trains took this loop — others reversed in Manningtree station.

This photo shows Class B12/3 4-6-0 L.N.E.R. No. 8559 leaving Manningtree on a Sunday afternoon Ipswich-Harwich train. It had just reversed. This photo was taken in October 1937.

Fig. 22 The purpose of building some branches now seems almost inexplicable, till one realizes that they were only a part of a more ambitious scheme which had to be abandoned when money ran out.

Such a branch ran from Haughley Junction to Laxfield. This had been built under the Light Railway Act of 1896 by the Mid Suffolk Light Railway, which always remained independent from The Great Eastern Railway. The original intention had been to build a line from Westerfield Junction through Debenham and Laxfield to Halesworth, with a branch from Kenton Junction to Haughley.

Work on the branch section started first. The opening of a new railway in Suffolk had always been the occasion for general rejoicing, but the Mid Suffolk Railway Company decided to have their feast when the first sod was cut at Westerfield, on 3rd May 1902. This ceremony was performed by H.R.H. The Duke of Cambridge and six hundred and two guests sat down to a magnificent luncheon. A patient of mine was a steward at these festivities.

No further progress was ever made at Westerfield.

On 23rd September 1902, Lord Kitchener, who had been staying nearby, paid a ceremonial visit to Mendlesham where the line from Haughley was under construction. He arrived by car. All the girls were in their best dresses and burst out clapping, saying "Bravo, Sir, Bravo". A patient of mine was one of them.

As could have been expected, the branch had a very stormy financial life. The village of Laxfield was reached on 20th September 1904 when the line was opened from Haughley for goods traffic. Passenger trains did not start running till 29th September 1908.

From 1906 till 1912 the line extended to Cratfield, a small village 2 miles beyond Laxfield, but was only used for freight services. From 1904 till 1906 a line was laid from Kenton Junction to a point near the village of Debenham. This was never officially opened, but does seem to have been used for freight (and the unofficial passenger).

Another patient of mine remembered seeing the two locomotives, which had been delivered to the line by Messrs. Hudswell Clarke in 1904, chained and padlocked to the rails at Haughley till the first instalment of their payment had been made.

The Mid Suffolk Light Railway, being independent, was always resented by the Great Eastern Railway. At the time of the 1923 grouping of the railway companies, the newly formed L.N.E.R. did not want anything to do with it. It was 1st July 1924 before it was finally foisted on to the L.N.E.R. owing, it was said in Laxfield, to the efforts of the local M.P. who, after a good lunch, informed the other members of the Parliamentary Committee considering the take over Bill, that Laxfield was a large thriving market town of great importance, which could not possibly be deprived of its vital railway. The other members did not like to admit that they had never heard of Laxfield, and so the branch became part of the L.N.E.R.

This photo shows Class J65 0-6-0T L.N.E.R. No. 7247 at Laxfield in March 1931 and shows the original lightly laid track with flat bottomed rails.

Fig. 21 Hadleigh, shown here on the occasion of a society visit in June 1956, was the terminus of a short seven mile branch from Bentley, between Manningtree and Ipswich. Although the track bed would have allowed it, there was never any through running from Ipswich. The branch was closed to passenger traffic on 29th February 1932. Freight traffic was considerable and lasted till 19th September 1965.

During the nineteen-fifties a special parcels train used to run every afternoon.

The locomotive pictured is Class J15 0-6-0 No. 65459.

▲ *Fig. 23* The engine shed at Laxfield in its last days, after a severe storm, in 1951.

Class J15 0-6-0 No. 65388, which at that time was working the three days a week freight train to Haughley and back, is stabled in the shed.

During the sugar beet season the freight train ran daily.

▼ *Fig. 24* The last train from Laxfield ran on Saturday 20th July 1952.

On 7th August 1952 Class J15 0-6-0 No. 65388 came down to Laxfield with the Colchester steam crane (with an Ipswich crew). This photo shows it removing the main water tank. Thanks to the efforts of Mr. D. W. Harvey, at the time Shed Master at Norwich, this tank now serves for the storage of water for the lavatories at Tan-y-Bwlch on the Festiniog Railway.

▲ *Fig. 25* This picture, also taken on 7th August 1952, shows Class J15 0-6-0 No. 65388 standing beside the pond which constituted the emergency locomotive water supply at Laxfield. It was situated near Laxfield Mill (the end of the line, half a mile beyond Laxfield station). The water was pumped up into a tank by a very ancient petrol engine.

No. 65388 had come on to the branch at Haughley at 6.30 a.m. that morning. It was now late afternoon and the driver was getting worried about his water supply. The fireman saw himself having to replenish the tender by bucket from the pond.

All telephones had been removed from the branch immediately after the closure. It was 8.30 p.m. that night before the anxious signalman at Haughley saw the train reappear.

▼ *Fig. 26* The Saturday afternoon train leaving Kenton Junction behind Class J15 0-6-0 No. 65467.

There was no school traffic from Stowmarket on Saturday afternoons, so the train started from Haughley. The only adult season ticket holder on the branch did not travel from Laxfield to Kenton and back on Saturdays. Thus some incredibly early arrivals used to be made at Laxfield on Saturday afternoons — except once when the guard was left behind at Wilby and the train had to reverse to pick him up.

▲ *Fig. 27* Kenton Junction was the only crossing place on the branch. Class J15 0-6-0 No. 65459 is approaching Kenton with the morning mixed train from Haughley.

On one occasion, when it had not been possible to lower the signal for six months, great consternation was caused on the station by the driver coming to a standstill and whistling. After a minute or two the station staff correctly decided that a V.I.P. might be on the train. What must have been an original Mid Suffolk Light Railway green flag was discovered, unfurled and freed from cobwebs. There was just enough material for the train to be waved in according to regulations.

The siding was the only surviving part of the line which had once nearly reached Debenham. Behind the buffer stops can be seen a water tank which was supplied from a pond, similar to that at Laxfield.

▼ *Fig. 28* The last freight train from Laxfield arriving at Brockford behind Class J15 0-6-0 No. 65388 on 25th July 1952. The distinctive station name board will be noticed. All the other station name boards were similar. They were made locally.

At the rear of the train is a tender which had once been attached to M. and G.N. 4-4-0 No. 25. It arrived at Laxfield on 1st January 1948 — the first day of British Railways — freshly painted L.N.E.R. It was used as a water carrier. It survived at Ipswich and Norwich till 1970, unfortunately missing preservation by only twenty-four hours. The M. and G.N. yellow paint was still well preserved when the overlying coats of black were gently rubbed away.

Driver Skinner and Fireman Law are on the footplate.

▲ *Fig. 29* During the 1939-45 war, airfields for the use of the United States forces were built at Horham and Mendlesham, on the Mid Suffolk Light Railway. To assist the working of the increased traffic, track alterations were carried out at Haughley. These allowed the branch line trains to use the main line station. The site of the original branch sidings, however, was via the 1 in 43 bank which the branch trains had to face immediately on leaving Haughley. The first quarter mile of the branch was strengthened to take main line locomotives capable of carrying out this shunting.

This photo shows class J39 0-6-0 No. 64829 shunting on the bank.

Driver Read of Laxfield told me that when the L.N.E.R. took over the Mid Suffolk Light Railway in 1924, a locomotive inspector soon came out from Ipswich. He did not like the traditional way of getting the small Hudswell Clarke tank engines up the bank and came back the next day to show how it should be done. He completely failed to get even half way up the bank, although he had several tries. The original locomotives were soon replaced by Class J65 0-6-0Ts, which in turn were replaced in 1947 by Class J15 0-6-0s, when all the original flat bottomed track had been removed.

▼ *Fig. 30* One of the results of the track alterations at Haughley was that the afternoon branch train started from Stowmarket, for the benefit of the Grammar School passengers. It had to reverse at Haughley from the down main line to the up main line in order to reach the branch.

Class J15 0-6-0 No. 65447 is coming up the main line from Stowmarket to Haughley. The six-wheeled coaches which formed its train are believed to have been the last in general use on British Railways. The train made a striking contrast with the Britannia hauled Norwich express which had preceded it up the bank.

Driver Rouse is on the footplate. He had transferred to Laxfield from Yorkshire where he had been the driver of the L.N.E.R. 2-8-0-0-8-2 Garrett banker on the Wath incline.

▲ *Fig. 31* By 1951 the roofs of the six-wheeled coaches were no longer water-tight. On very wet days a bogie coach had to be detached at Haughley from a passing local for use on the branch. In October 1951 the old coaches were replaced by four ex-suburban coaches displaced by the recent electrification.

Class J15 0-6-0 No. 65447 is entering Stradbroke with one set of these coaches.

◄ *Fig. 32* Class J15 0-6-0 No. 65456 is entering Haughley on a Bury St. Edmunds-Ipswich local train.

In the exchange sidings is a Class J19 0-6-0 which had become a total failure the previous night.

▲ *Fig. 33* Haughley had been a junction station since 1848 — sixty years before the opening to passenger traffic of the Mid Suffolk Light Railway.

Here a Norwich-Ipswich local train enters Haughley behind B17/6 3 cylinder 4-6-0 No. 61637 *"Thorpe Hall"*. Class J39 0-6-0 No. 64841 has just come in from the Bury St. Edmunds branch on a freight train and has been routed into the up loop. On more than one occasion the locomotive had been unable to control its train on the bank leading down from the Bury direction to the main line and had crashed through the railings, overturning on the public road.

▼ *Fig. 34* The Eastern Union Railway linking Ipswich with Norwich reached Mellis in 1849. The three mile branch from Mellis to Eye was opened in 1867. In 1861 Eye had a population of 2,430.

Class J17 0-6-0 No. 65553 is shunting at Eye in 1958.

Seasonal produce trains used to be run through to London from Eye.

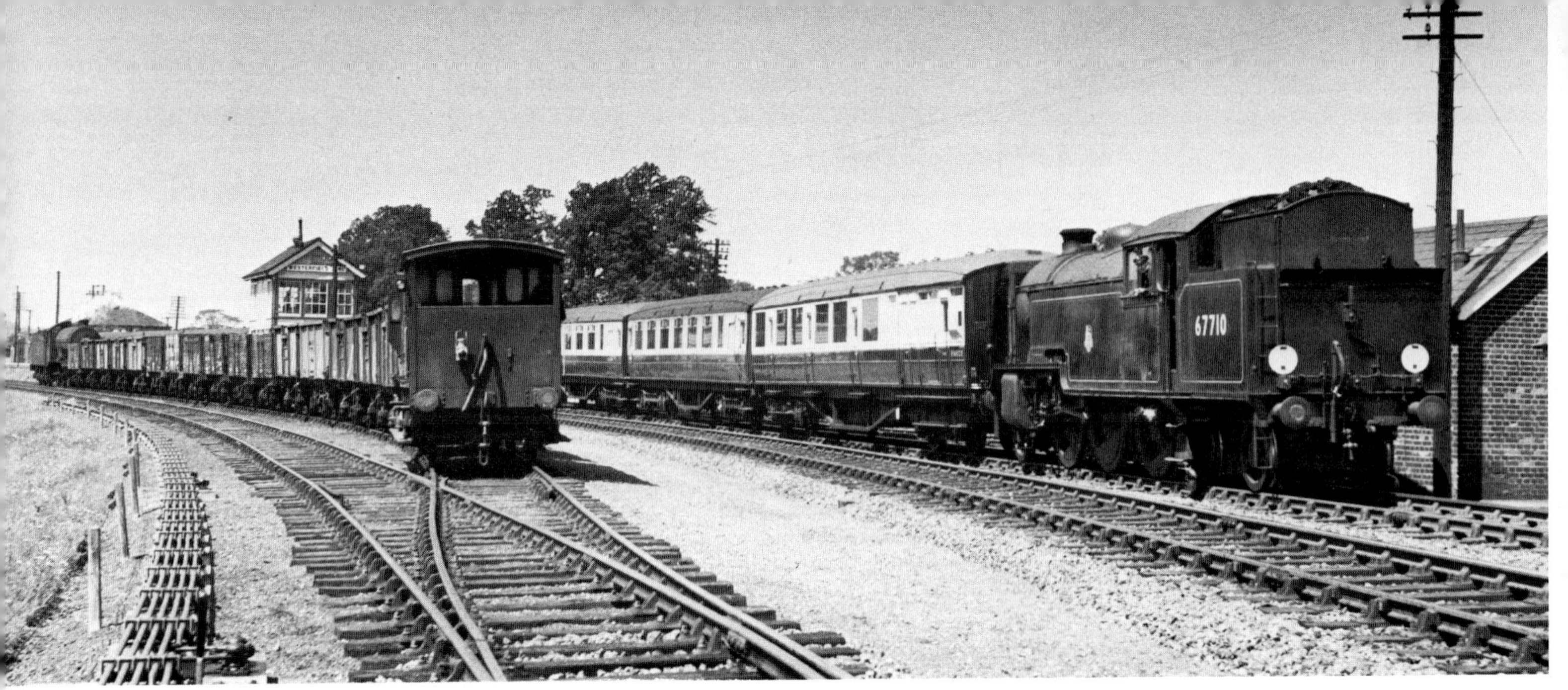
67710

6127
No 6127

L N E R
8574

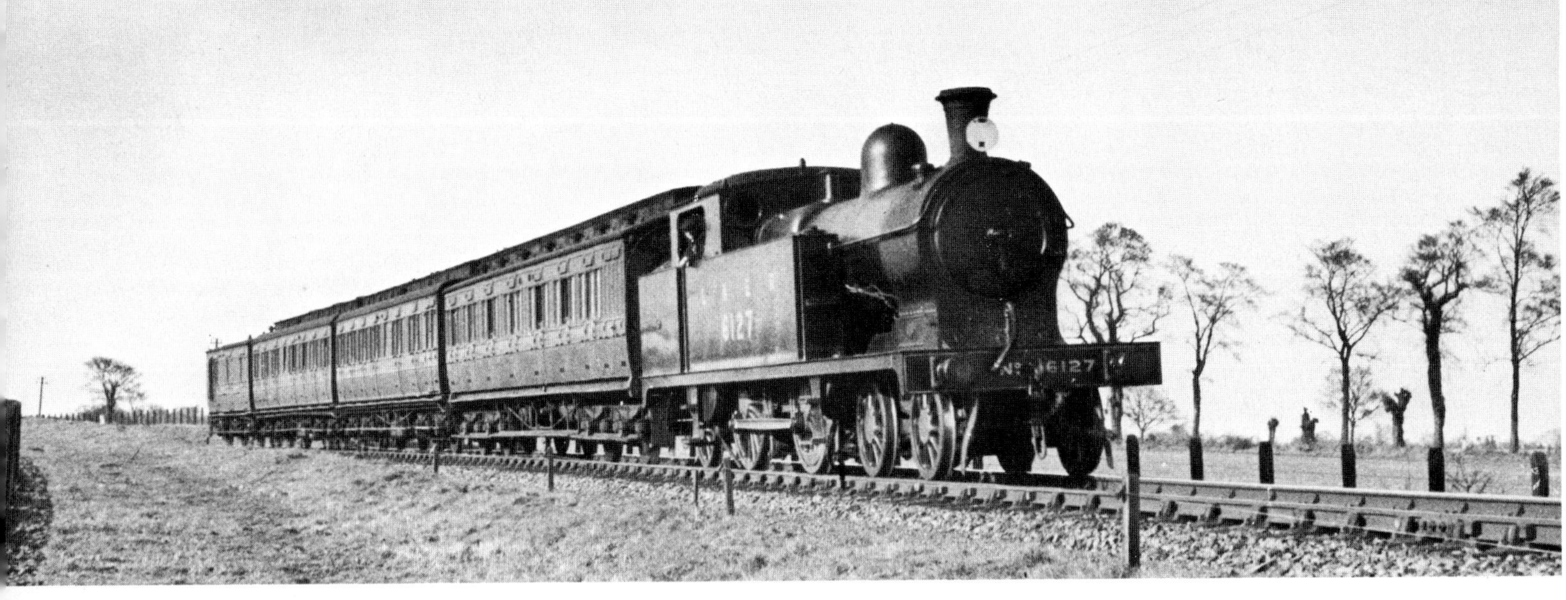

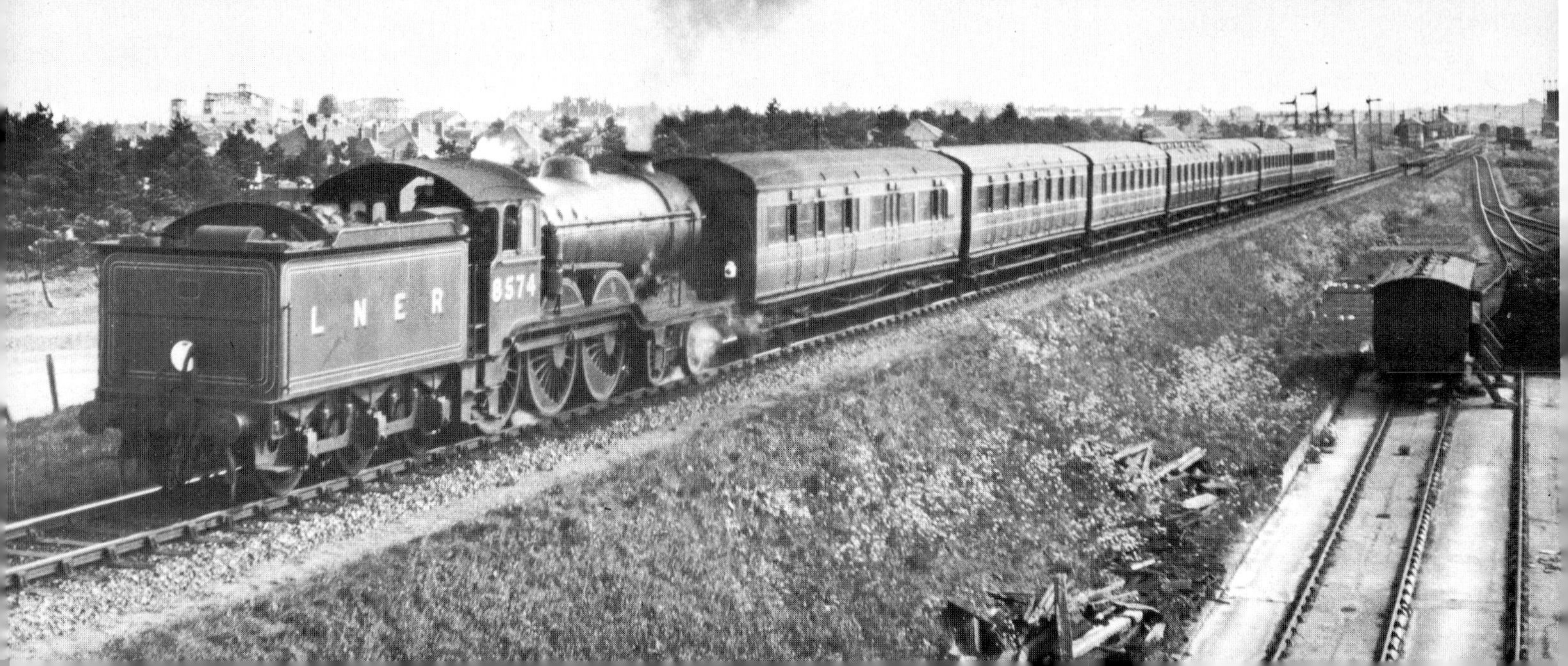

Fig. 35 In 1861 the population of Felixstow (as it was then spelled) was 673 and that of the combined parishes of Trimley, 967. Yet Col. Tomline, a local landowner, had the imagination to build a branch line from Westerfield Junction, on the East Suffolk line, to Felixstowe Dock, which was opened in 1877. The Great Eastern Railway took over the working of the branch in 1879 and bought it in 1887.

Class L1 2-6-4T No. 67710 is coming on to the branch at Westerfield Junction on a through summer Saturday express from Liverpool Street. Locomotives had been changed at Ipswich. A Class J39 9-6-0 is standing in the original branch station on a local freight train, waiting for a path to Ipswich.

Fig. 38 There were two common reasons for building a branch line. The first, which does not apply to East Anglia, is a hilly terrain, where the railway can only go so far up a valley before being stopped by the hills or mountains. The second, which applied all over the country, was the objection by influential local landowners to a railway running through their property.

It was the original intention to take the East Suffolk line from Woodbridge through Framlingham and on to Halesworth.

But as the Duke of Hamilton objected to the line traversing his property at Easton, Framlingham had to be served by a branch which left the East Suffolk line at Wickham Market Junction, one mile from Wickham Market for Campsea Ashe station. This station was situated two miles from the village of Wickham Market (Campsea Ashe only had a population of 379 in 1861), and so, like so many other places, could not hope to compete when local bus services started to run.

This photo shows Class J15 0-6-0 No. 65433 coming off the Framlingham branch on to the main line at Wickham Market Junction. The fireman is giving up the staff which weighed eight pounds and which often severely bruised the fireman's or signalman's arm. The staff was made of brass and carried the Annetts Key which unlocked the points at intermediate stations.

Fig. 36 The Felixstowe branch was always difficult to work on account of the extreme seasonal variation in traffic. Because of the exposed nature of the line, a tank locomotive was always used if available.

In April 1936, Class C14 4-4-2T L.N.E.R. No. 6127 is shown on the branch train near Derby Road. Locomotives of this ex-Great Central Railway class had recently arrived at Ipswich and remained on the branch for the next fifteen years.

The train is composed of an ex-North Eastern Railway clerestory bogie next to the engine, followed by two ex-Great Eastern Railway clerestory bogies.

About this time the older Great Eastern Railway six-wheeled vehicles were being replaced by these ex-North Eastern Railway bogies.

Fig. 37 Felixstowe owes much to the Great Eastern Railway for its development. Through trains and coaches were run to Liverpool Street and this photo, taken in September 1937, shows Class B12/3 4-6-0 L.N.E.R. No. 8574 leaving Felixstowe Beach on the Sunday afternoon through express to Liverpool Street. The train had to reverse at Felixstowe Town. The corridor clerestory coach (fourth from the locomotive) had been built in 1904 for use on the Liverpool Street-Parkeston Quay boat express.

In the foreground are the foundations of a carriage painting shed which had been destroyed by fire.

Fig. 39 Class B12/3 4-6-0 No. 61561 is coming off the branch with a through Sunday excursion from Framlingham to Liverpool Street. The train joined up at Ipswich with another excursion from Norwich or Bury St. Edmunds.

Fig. 40 A Sunday excursion from Framlingham to Liverpool Street pauses at Hacheston Halt, behind Class J15 0-6-0 No. 65447. Because main line stock had to be used on these trains, the Framlingham Station Master's pair of household steps was carried in the guard's van. A passenger is joining the train, climbing up the steps assisted by a helping hand from the guard and carefully watched by the fireman. The driver is supervising this unusual procedure from the footplate.

Great skill was required when returning at night in the darkness.

When Queen Victoria used to travel in her non-corridor Royal train to and from Scotland, it used to be halted at a lonely spot near Beattock so that her ladies-in-waiting could be changed. They, too, had to climb in and out of the Royal train by means of a similar pair of steps.

Fig. 41 Economies introduced in the nineteen-thirties required the train crew to open and shut a pair of level crossing gates near Marlesford. If this procedure was not carried out too quickly, there was time for the driver to collect enough watercress from beside the railway bank for his supper.

This photo, taken in August 1936, shows the rare visit of a main line locomotive to the branch, after a derailment. It shows Class D16/3 4-4-0 L.N.E.R. No. 8855, waiting for the level crossing gates to be opened.

The train is the standard branch line train of the period — two six-wheeled gas-lit passenger coaches and a six-wheeled van.

▲ *Fig. 42* This photo taken in 1949, shows the Framlingham branch train between Marlesford and Hacheston Halt, hauled by Class F3 2-4-2T No. 67127.

The old six-wheeled coaches were replaced in May 1940 by bogie coaches, which had originally been built in 1907, for the Norfolk Coast Express. As with the old six-wheeled stock, a pair of steps could be lowered automatically by the guard for passengers using Hacheston Halt.

The morning train in the last few years of the branch was always mixed — sometimes quite a heavy load was conveyed. Freight traffic for Parham was dealt with by the midday mixed train returning from Framlingham and sometimes trucks for Marlesford would be propelled in the afternoon down from Wickham Market. It was possible to take the midday train to Wickham Market and then to have lunch in the restaurant car on the connecting up Yarmouth train between there and Ipswich.

In the 1861 census the population of Marlesford was 526. Although it always remained a small village, at the turn of the century a staff of seven were employed at the station.

▼ *Fig. 43* The morning mixed train is shown between Parham and Framlingham hauled by Class D16/2 4-4-0 No. 62590.

▲ *Fig. 44* Class J15 0-6-0 No. 65445 shunting the daily freight train at Framlingham.

As at so many similar busy country goods yards, till the nineteen-twenties, the yard shunting was performed by a horse.

▼ *Fig. 45* Another view of the yard at Framlingham. It is of extreme interest in showing Class J15 0-6-0 No. 65454 on its final duty.

On 10th May 1959 a Sunday morning exercise was arranged for the county rescue services, involving a simulated train crash. Casualties were provided by members of the St. John's Ambulance Brigade and they lay about the two condemned coaches (seen in the siding) in a most realistic manner. No. 65454 at the head of these vehicles helped to bring home to all those taking part the grim horror of disaster. On 19th May 1959, after refilling its tender which had leaked away all its water, No. 65454 left for Ipswich piloting the freight train. Later that day she ran up light engine to Stratford for withdrawal.

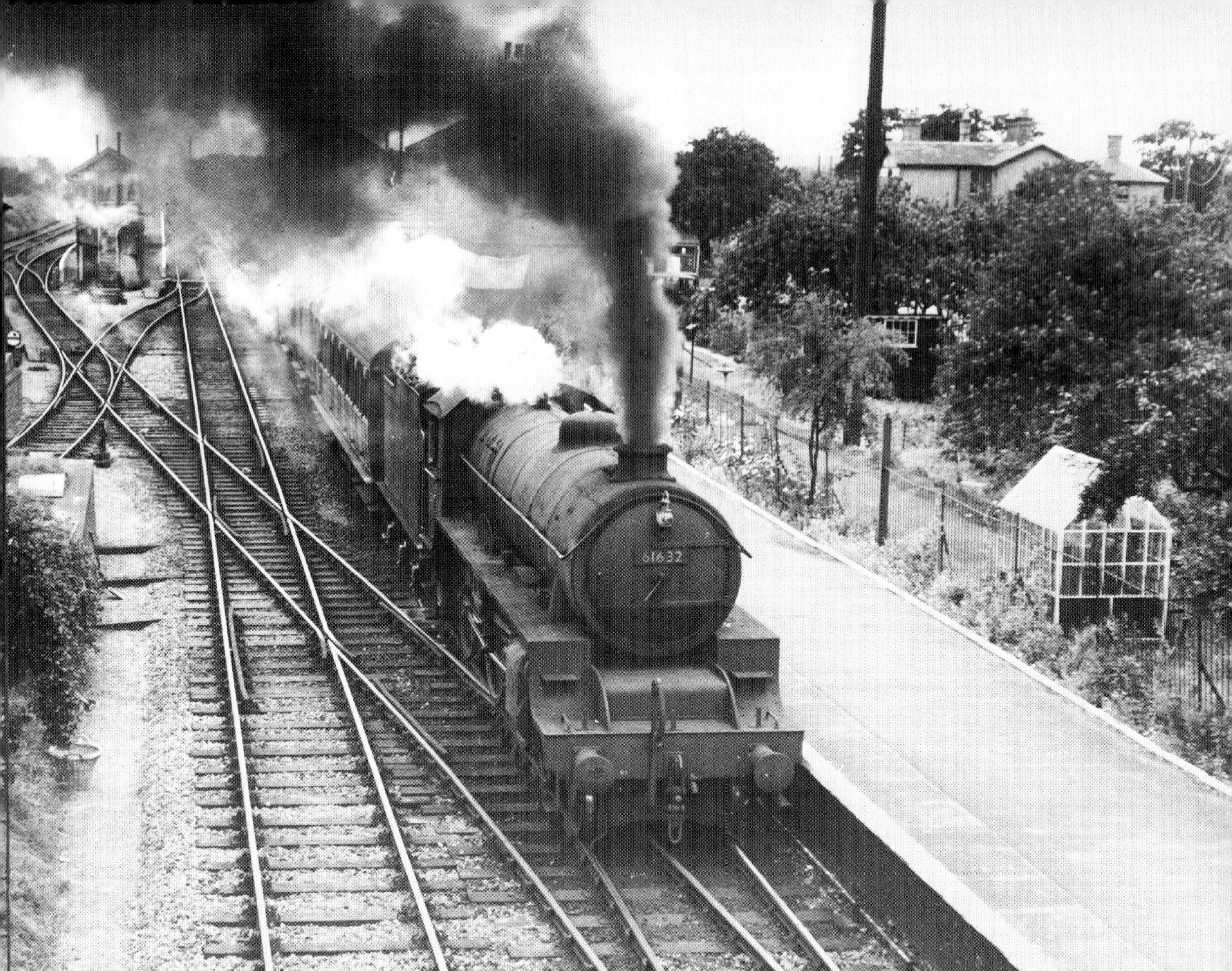

▲ *Fig. 46* At Wickham Market the Framlingham branch train ran through the station on the main line, and then reversed into the up bay platform. This was very low, and if necessary, the porter would bring a pair of steps to help passengers alight. In the down direction the train always departed from the main line.

This photo shows the very rare visit of a Class B2 4-6-0 No. 61632 *"Belvoir Castle"* to Wickham Market, on an Ipswich-Yarmouth South Town local train.

In October 1958 No. 61632 was renamed *"Royal Sovereign"* and was used as the Royal engine till it was withdrawn in February 1959.

Fig. 47 Thanks to a well-directed, vigorous local opposition, the East Suffolk line from Ipswich to Lowestoft was saved from Dr. Beeching's axe. It must now, however, be regarded only as a local pay-train branch line.

This picture, taken in August 1936, shows it in better days. Class B12 4-6-0 L.N.E.R. No. 8534 is seen approaching Wickham Market on an up Yarmouth South Town-Ipswich local.

The train is composed of an assortment of old Great Eastern Railway coaches.

At times of heavy passenger traffic, main line trains were still being strengthened by old Great Eastern Railway six-wheeled coaches.

I can remember travelling in a six-wheeled coach in July 1936, marshalled next to a Sandringham class 4-6-0 on an up express from Ipswich. It went through Witham at 80 m.p.h.

Fig. 48 A short freight branch ran from Snape Junction, between Wickham Market and Saxmundham, down to the Snape Maltings. Snape was built with a typical station house and was shown in the 1859 timetable, but without a passenger service. It never had one.

Here a Society special on the branch is being propelled back to the junction by Class E4 2-4-0 No. 62797. It was stopped by signal on the 1 in 53 gradient and could not restart. A Class J15 0-6-0 was sent down to the rescue.

▲ *Fig. 49* At Snape the river was crossed by an old Great Eastern Railway wooden trestle bridge, which normally was only traversed by Class J15 0-6-0s. Snape was not connected by phone to any signal box, so the foreman in charge never knew when the freight train was coming. The train was a "bonus train", always in a hurry, and propelled down from the junction very smartly. On occasions it arrived when the foreman was swimming in the river. There was not time for him to dress before dealing with the train.

Class J15 9-6-0 No. 65447 is leaving for Ipswich in 1959. By the time it had left Woodbridge, especially in the sugar beet season, it had usually collected a long and heavy train.

▼ *Fig. 50* In 1946-47, after the war, Ipswich did not always have a Class J15 0-6-0 available for the Snape goods. When this happened, a Class J17 was used, which left any trucks for Snape up at the junction siding. The Framlingham branch locomotive would then be sent for to take the trucks down to the Maltings. As the Framlingham branch locomotive at this time was usually a Class F3 2-4-2T, whose route availability was "3", special authorisation had to be given for it to work over a route availability "2" line.

In this photo the Framlingham branch locomotive Class F3 2-4-2T L.N.E.R. No. 7143 is shown leaving Snape, with Driver Bloom on the footplate.

The previous day, No. 7143 had been called on at Wickham Market to take over a Yarmouth Express from an ailing Class B12/3 4-6-0. She had acquitted herself very well and was turned at Yarmouth, before returning light engine to Framlingham. She is thus shown working chimney first in the up direction. This was extremely rare as it was the invariable rule for all branch line locomotives working from small country out-sheds to work chimney first in the down direction to facilitate coaling at night by hand.

▲ *Fig. 51* During the summer, between the two wars, a Pullman train called "The Eastern Belle" used to run from Liverpool Street to various resorts. Aldeburgh was visited in August and in 1938 a Sandringham class 4-6-0 hauled the train, managing the 1 in 53 gradient up from Saxmundham junction box without difficulty.

In August 1939, Class B12/3 4-6-0 L.N.E.R. No. 8577 had made a fast trip down to Saxmundham where it had to wait twenty minutes for the Aldeburgh branch train to come off the single track. On restarting she was soon in trouble on the 1 in 53 gradient and this photo shows the last puff of steam from her chimney before she stalled.

▼ *Fig. 52* Special workings over branch lines often presented problems for the operating staff. Here another Class B12/3 4-6-0 No. 61561 is in trouble at Saxmundham Junction, in August 1957. It was working the annual special train from Ipswich for the Aldeburgh Regatta.

The fireman has failed to take the staff from the signalman at the junction box. The signalman had to stand with the staff, at track level, while the driver wanted as much speed as possible to help get up the bank. The train is making an emergency stop, as it is in the single line section, without the authority of the staff. The fireman is waiting for the train to stop before going back to get the staff which the signalman is picking up from the ground.

▲ *Fig. 53* Class L1 2-6-4T No. 67705 is propelling the Ipswich six-wheeled officers' inspection saloon into Leiston. The booked locomotive had failed at the last moment and No. 67705 was the only one available. It could not proceed to Aldeburgh as arranged, because this section of track was route availability "4", while the L1s were route availability "7".

There were extensive sidings at Leiston chiefly for Richard Garrett's engineering works, seen to the right of the photo.

Fig. 54 Three Class F6 2-4-2Ts were stationed at Ipswich after ▶ they had been displaced from the London suburban services by the 1947 electrification. Of these, No. 67220 was the usual Aldeburgh branch locomotive, while No. 67230 was usually at work on the Framlingham branch. Here No. 67220 is leaving Thorpeness Halt on its journey from Saxmundham to Aldeburgh.

Fig. 55 On summer Saturdays a tender locomotive had to be ▶ provided for the Aldeburgh branch, so that the main line at Saxmundham would not be blocked while a tank locomotive was taking water. Class J15 0-6-0 No. 65467 is entering Aldeburgh on a summer Saturday morning.

▲ *Fig. 56* In August 1955, two ex-suburban tank locomotives, Class F6 2-4-2T No. 67223 (train locomotive) and Class F5 2-4-2T No. 67201 (pilot) double-head a Beccles-Lowestoft local train.

British Rail continued to the end the Great Eastern Railway practice of conveying through coaches for Yarmouth South Town and Lowestoft on all London expresses, the Lowestoft coaches being either attached or detached at Beccles.

When the Yarmouth and Lowestoft coaches were combined at Ipswich with those from Norwich, some very heavy trains ensued for the journey to Liverpool Street, which, until 1928, had to be hauled by the Class B12 4-6-0s.

▼ *Fig. 57* At Oulton Broad South a short freight branch diverged, and after a couple of miles, divided into three.

One line ran to the coal depot at Kirkley, one ran to the South Harbour at Lowestoft and the third ran down the side of a busy road to serve the Co-operative Society's factory and Boulton and Paul's timber yard.

In this photo Class J15 0-6-0 No. 65389 is coming in with coal truck empties from Kirkley. It has left the rest of its train on the South Harbour line.

Class J17 0-6-0 No. 65559 is standing on the third line with a ballast train.

Fig. 58 Class J15 0-6-0 No. 65460 after picking up trucks from ▶ the Co-operative Society's factory at Lowestoft. Three busy roads joined here and there was always a fascinated audience for the passage of the train, protected by the man with a red flag. The train is returning to Oulton Broad South, having served Boulton and Paul's timber yard and the Co-operative Society's oil siding.

Fig. 59 An oddity on the freight branch from Oulton Broad ▶ South was a double fixed home signal of Great Eastern Railway origin. Class J15 0-6-0 No. 65478 is passing this signal, necessarily at danger, on its way back to Oulton Broad South.

A few years before the closure of this branch, the signal arms were replaced by those of a standard British Rail pattern. The post with its finial was still retained.

BERNEY ARMS

◀ *Fig. 60* In 1903 The Norfolk and Suffolk Joint Committee opened a coast line between Yarmouth Beach and Lowestoft, with a spur from Yarmouth South Town, which was Great Eastern Railway property.

Traffic on this line was never heavy and on 21st September 1953, was restricted to the section from Yarmouth South Town, the line from Yarmouth Beach being severed. On the closure of the main line from Beccles to Yarmouth South Town via Haddiscoe, on 2nd November 1959, Yarmouth traffic was sent via Lowestoft and the coastal branch line was brought up to the main line standard. Passengers would not pay the increased fare caused by this diversion and in 1966 the branch, which for six years had become a main line, reverted to a single track branch, finally being closed completely on 4th May 1970.

This photo shows Class N7/3 0-6-2T No. 69708 on a Yarmouth South Town-Lowestoft push and pull train leaving Lowestoft North. The spacious layout, typical of this branch, will be noted.

During the nineteen-fifties, camping coaches were placed at all the stations on the branch, one of them being the Pullman car "Grosvenor", which had been built in 1908 for "The Brighton Belle".

◀ *Fig. 61* The building of branch lines in the area covered by the waterways of the Norfolk Broads was influenced (as was the building of roads) by the marshy ground and the sites where it

was possible to build bridges.

In August 1954 Class D16/3 4-4-0 No. 62611 is entering Berney Arms station which was still lit by paraffin lamps, on the single track branch from Reedham Junction to Yarmouth Vauxhall.

This line carried a dense traffic on summer Saturdays.

▲ *Fig. 62* Trains from Norwich to Yarmouth Vauxhall could also travel via the single line branch through Acle, and in view of the complexity of the local services, trains from Norwich carried route indicating headcodes.

This photo shows class J39 0-6-0 No. 64726 on a Norwich-Yarmouth Vauxhall train via Acle, at Breydon Junction. The route indicating headcode will be noticed.

▼ *Fig. 63* In May 1937, Class E4 2-4-0 L.N.E.R. No. 7501 is about to leave Yarmouth Vauxhall on a local train to Norwich, routed via Reedham Junction.

▲ *Fig. 64* A freight tramway ran through the streets of Yarmouth from Vauxhall station to the Fishmarket. This line cut right across the main traffic centre in Yarmouth and this photo, taken from the footplate of Drewry Class 04 No. D2210, shows a most unusual scene.

The driver commented: "The police have tidy minds — they don't like seeing us charging across their one way traffic system like this".

This line survived till the end of 1975.

▼ *Fig. 65* The tramway from Yarmouth Quay to the Fishmarket became impossible to use in the late nineteen-sixties. Parked cars on the track were causing complete blockage.

Access to and from the Quay was also similarly impeded, but the train staff became very adept at shifting parked cars or finding their owners. On the occasion when I took this photo, the train was held up for forty-five minutes because a lady journalist, who had parked her car in the middle of the track, was under an anaesthetic in a nearby dentist's surgery. It shows B.R. Drewry Class 04 No. D2212 on the quay at Yarmouth.

Gresley Pacifics, many various classes of Great Western Railway locomotives, including Counties and Castles, and various Southern Railway moguls and Bulleid 0-6-0s, all made their last journey in England along the tramway to Yarmouth Quay. Probably of these, Castle Class 4-6-0 No. 7017 *"G. J. Churchward"* had borne the most distinguished name. They were on their way to Belgium, in trucks, as scrap, after being cut up by Kings of Norwich.

▲ *Fig. 66* In 1882 the Yarmouth Union Railway built a short branch from Yarmouth Beach Station to join the Great Eastern Railway tramway to the Fish Quay. The junction with the latter was at North Quay, in the middle of a public road. This connecting branch subsequently became part of the M. and G.N.

Taken in October 1967 Class 04 Drewry shunter No. D2210 trundles through The Hole in the Wall — a narrow passage between the White Swan public house and the adjacent property, with a load of coal trucks for the White Swan coal depot.

After the closure of the M. and G.N. on 2nd March 1959, this traffic (and that for the Co-operative Society's coal depot situated a quarter of a mile beyond the White Swan depot) had to be routed via Yarmouth Vauxhall and North Quay Junction, where a reversal was necessary. On one occasion, at least, this route was taken by an officers' inspection saloon.

Class J65 0-6-0T No. 68214 survived at Yarmouth Beach till October 1956 as spare engine for use on the Quay lines. This had survived three years after all the other members of the class had been withdrawn.

▼ *Fig. 67* The Midland and Great Northern Railway, mostly situated in North Norfolk, was the only competitor to the Great Eastern Railway's monopoly in East Anglia. It was originally formed by the fusion of several small branches into a main line system which connected with the Midland Railway at Saxby, near Leicester, and with the Great Northern Railway at Peterborough and Spalding.

One of the earliest of these branches was opened in 1876 and ran from Yarmouth Beach to Stalham.

In August 1949, Class K2 2-6-0 No. 61748 hauls a summer Saturday express from the Midlands to Yarmouth Beach and Lowestoft, near Stalham.

On the closure of the M. and G.N. system on 2nd March 1959, all its traffic was routed into Yarmouth Vauxhall, via Norwich.

Fig. 69 Britannia class 4-6-2 No. 70006 *"Robert Burns"* passes Haddiscoe Low Level station on a Wester- ▶
field Junction-Norwich football special, in April 1957.

Passenger trains over this loop were very rare — only when the main line from Norwich to Ipswich was
completely blocked. It was used by freight trains and for locomotive operating purposes.

It had been used by passenger trains from Beccles from 1854 till 1859, before the line from Haddiscoe
to Yarmouth South Town was completed, and again in 1925, when the Haddiscoe swing bridge was renewed.

No. 70006, Robert Burns, was one of the famous Norwich Britannias which will always be associated
with Bill Harvey.

▲ *Fig. 68* At Haddiscoe the Great Eastern main line from Beccles to
Yarmouth South Town, which was closed to all traffic on 2nd
November 1959, crossed over the line from Norwich to Lowestoft.
There was consequently a High Level and Low Level station.

Here Class D16/3 4-4-0 No. 62524 is propelling an officer's
special from Yarmouth South Town to Norwich, through
Haddiscoe High Level station.

Fleet Junction signalbox can be seen in the background where
the train reversed on to the loop which ran down to the Low
Level station. The signal on this loop can be seen between the
railway houses.

In the immediate foreground another loop once ran down to
Marsh Junction. This was opened in 1872 and allowed a
Yarmouth South Town-Lowestoft through service (the direct
coast line between these two places was not opened till 1903).

This service was withdrawn on 8th September 1934 and the track
taken up in January 1939.

This photo which had to be taken direct into the sun, was
helped by a partial eclipse. A down express had just passed and
the signals are returning to danger.

Fig. 70 Class A5 4-6-2T No. 69826 is leaving Reedham Junction ▶
on the Lowestoft portion of the through train from York to
Yarmouth and Lowestoft.

In the background can be seen the track bed of the East
curve at Reedham Junction. This was used in the eighteen-fifties
by a through service from Yarmouth Vauxhall to Lowestoft and
again in 1925 by the East Suffolk line trains from Ipswich to
Yarmouth, while the swing bridge at Haddiscoe was being renewed.

Fig. 71 Aldeby station, between Beccles and Haddiscoe, remained open for sugar beet traffic till February 1965.

In November 1960, Class J17 0-6-0 No. 65567 is leaving Aldeby for Haddiscoe Low Level with a train of sugar beet, on the up line.

St. Olave's station, the other side of the river at Haddiscoe, remained open till the end of the sugar beet season, in January 1960, the train working from Yarmouth South Town.

Fig. 72 From Beccles, The Waveney Valley branch ran across to Tivetshall, on the Norwich-Ipswich main line.

In June 1951, a Tivetshall-Yarmouth South Town Sunday excursion pulls out of Ellingham. The locomotive, Class J15 0-6-0 No. 65469, was in difficulties with its heavy load and a pilot locomotive had to be sent for from Lowestoft to assist from Beccles.

It was a sweltering hot day and the swing bridge at Beccles jammed. The train had, therefore, to make a long detour via Lowestoft and Haddiscoe Low Level to reach Yarmouth.

All subsequent Sunday excursions over this branch were always double headed from Norwich.

▲ *Fig. 73* At Pulham Market a short branch, owned by the Air Ministry, led up to an airfield associated with airship development — notably the R33.

This photo shows Class N7/3 0-6-2T No. 69679 coming off the branch in June 1957.

The Waveney Valley branch carried a very heavy traffic during the 1939-45 war and the airfield at Pulham was used for R.A.F. stores throughout the nineteen-fifties.

The section of the branch from Beccles to Ditchingham was officially closed on 19th April 1965, but as the siding at Coltishall was not ready to receive the Pointer block trains of sand which were then working from Ditchingham, in practice it remained open till August 1965.

▼▲ *Figs. 74 and 75* Class J15 0-6-0 No. 65471 carries out shunting operations at Pulham airfield in December 1957. The R.A.F. base was closed in February 1958.

Fig. 76 Class F4 2-4-2T No. 67167 accelerates away from Homersfield on a Beccles-Tivetshall train in 1950.

Passenger services were closed on the branch on 5th January 1953.

Owing to the weak bridge over the River Waveney at Beccles, the through trains from Norwich were normally restricted to Class E4 2-4-0s or Class J15 0-6-0s and the local service from Beccles to Tivetshall to Class F4 or F4 2-4-2Ts. As on the Maldon branch, Class F6 2-4-2Ts were not allowed.

Fig. 77 The cross-country branch from County School to Wroxham was closed to passenger traffic on 15th September 1952 and the track taken up between Foulsham and Reepham, part of the bed being sold.

The closure of the M. and G.N. line on 2nd March 1959 found Norwich City still with a heavy freight traffic. To work this economically it was necessary to reinstate the branch line from Reepham to Themelthorpe, where a new curve was opened on 12th September 1960, which joined the M. and G.N. line from Norwich City to the Wroxham branch.

This photo shows Class E4 2-4-0 No. 62787 entering Aylsham on a Norwich to Norwich train, via Wymondham, Dereham, County School and Wroxham. By taking a 3s. 3d. return cheap day ticket from Norwich to Foulsham, it was possible to travel from Norwich to Norwich without changing. I once met a fellow passenger who claimed it was his third time round — all for 3s. 3d.!

▲ *Fig. 78* Class E4 2-4-0 No. 62792 at Aylsham; Class J17 0-6-0 No. 65513 is in the bay, with a short freight train.

The traditional branch line van is still marshalled in the train next to the locomotive.

▼ *Fig. 79* Class J15 0-6-0 No. 65472 returns to Norwich with the breakdown train after helping to rerail a Class J39 0-6-0 at Fellingham on the M. and G.N. It is reversing from North Walsham Town (M. and G.N.) to Antingham Road Junction on the North Walsham main — Mundesley-Cromer Beach line. After a further reversal at the junction it had a through run back to Norwich.

▶ *Fig. 80* In 1957 an overbridge on the loop shown in the previous photo needed renewal. Instead, a new connection was built south of North Walsham main station and this photo, taken in October 1958, shows Class B1 4-6-0 No. 61001 *"Eland"* transferring a truck, by means of this new connection, from North Walsham Main to the goods yard at North Walsham Town.

The only passenger trains to use this new line were the Holiday Camps Expresses, which made one trip in each direction on Saturdays only, during the 1958 summer train service.

The goods yards at North Walsham have now been adapted to deal with North Sea oil trains. (For a short time these had been dealt with at Coltishall).

▼ *Fig. 81* About the turn of the century, Cromer and Shering-ham became fashionable holiday resorts. In 1907 the Great Eastern Railway built a complete new train which ran non-stop from Liverpool Street to North Walsham, to serve these towns. It was called "The Norfolk Coast Express".

In September 1928 Class B12 4-6-0 L.N.E.R. No. 1552 is working this train over the single line section near Gunton.

▲ *Fig. 84* Unusual use for a branch line was that at Wymondham, where a short section of the line to Forncett, on the main Norwich-Ipswich line, had been left, when the rest of the branch was closed to all traffic in 1951. (Passenger traffic had been withdrawn on 10th September 1939).

During the mid nineteen-sixties, hundreds of redundant British Rail passenger coaches were gutted by fire at a lonely spot two miles down the branch. The frames were then taken on to Kings of Norwich to be broken up for scrap.

This photo shows three Pullman cars, originally built for the 1933 electrification from London to Brighton, on their way to be gutted. They were "Daisy", "Olive", and "Peggy" and were being propelled by class 03 No. D2018 in October 1967.

▼ *Fig. 85* One of the few remaining Class D13 4-4-0s, L.N.E.R. No. 8030 is in charge of a Wells-next-the-Sea to Norwich train, near Wymondham in June 1937.

The D13s had originally been built as 2-4-0s between 1886 and 1897.

◄ *Fig. 82* Trains which carried through coaches for Sheringham (like "The Norfolk Coast Express") stopped at Cromer Junction signal box, seen in the background of this photo. Here they were detached and, after the main train had proceeded to Cromer High, a locomotive which had been waiting by the signal box took them on to Sheringham.

A Liverpool St.-Cromer High express is hauled from Norwich by a L.M.S. type 2-6-4T No. 42221 which was working experimentally from Norwich for a few months in 1954.

◄ *Fig. 83* Trains from Sheringham stopped at Cromer Junction box and then reversed into Cromer High station.

Such a train is being propelled into Cromer High by Class B17/6 3 cylinder 4-6-0 No. 61665 *"Leicester City"*. The calling on signal was "off" (it must have been very difficult for the driver to see).

Cromer High was situated high up outside the town and was closed to passenger traffic in September 1954. After this date the trains were routed into the much more centrally placed Cromer Beach station — the former M. & G.N. terminus.

▲ *Fig. 86* Class D16/3 4-4-0 No. 62570 waits at Dereham on a Wells-next-the-Sea to Norwich train in 1953. Standing beside it is Class E4 2-4-0 No. 62792 which has just backed on to a train from Norwich and is about to leave for Kings Lynn via Swaffham.

▼ *Fig. 87* Class D15/2 4-4-0 No. 62509 reverses out of Dereham station, after arriving from Kings Lynn.
   The locomotive was withdrawn in September 1952, a few weeks after this photo was taken. It was the last of the unrebuilt Claud Hamilton 4-4-0s to remain in service.

▲ *Fig. 88* Dereham station could be avoided by using a loop which allowed through running from Norwich to Kings Lynn. In practice it was chiefly used for turning locomotives, though on occasions it was taken by summer excursion from Kings Lynn to Yarmouth.

Class J19 9-6-0 No. 64640 is shown on this loop with a freight train for Kings Lynn.

Dereham locomotive shed can be seen to the left of the buffer beam.

▼ *Fig. 89* In August 1960 Class J15 0-6-0 No. 65469 enters Dereham on the North Elmham milk train.

The extent of the traffic once handled by the railway can be seen by the sidings serving two granaries. There was also a large yard to the south of the station and another to the west.

The old fashioned milk churn had long since disappeared and milk was conveyed, as by road, in large tanks.

Fig. 90 County School was the junction for the branch to Wroxham, which ran parallel to the line to Wells-next-the-Sea for about a mile before curving round to the east, and always remained a perfect unspoiled example of a Great Eastern country junction station.

Here Class J17 0-6-0 No. 65571 is leaving County School with a train of sugar beet.

▲ *Fig. 91* In 1857 the line from Norwich, which had reached Fakenham in 1849, was opened to Wells-next-the-Sea. In 1860 a short branch to the harbour was constructed and in 1866 the branch to Heacham Junction on the Kings Lynn-Hunstanton line was opened.

In consequence, the station at Wells-next-the-Sea always had a very interesting lay-out, seen here in 1960 with Class J17 0-6-0 No. 65583 simmering in the background.

The last passenger train over the branch from Heacham was an excursion conveying pilgrims from Northampton to Walsingham on Sunday, 11th June 1952. It arrived behind a Class B12/3 4-6-0, but the train was too long to allow the two waiting Class D16/3 4-4-0s to be attached. It had to be split and worked forward to Walsingham in two halves.

There was a section of track near Burnham Market which retained Great Eastern Railway 1877 rails till it was taken up.

No 7485

7485

▲ *Fig. 94* In August 1936 Class J18 0-6-0 L.N.E.R. No. 8141 heads a cattle train near Roudham Junction.

Roudham Junction was an exchange platform which could be used to allow the Swaffham-Thetford branch train to make a connection with a train for Norwich. At one time it was regularly used thus by the last evening train. It was not shown in the public time table, but all the branch trains stopped to serve the few railwaymen's houses. Tickets issued to Roudham Junction from Thetford were still printed L.N.E.R. when the Swaffham branch closed on 15th June 1964.

In an agricultural area, the staff of any branch line had to be able to deal with the problems caused by the arrival or despatch of a cattle train. The cattle had to be fed and watered periodically and after use, the cattle trucks had to be hosed down. The cattle dock was an integral part of all branch line stations.

▼ *Fig. 95* Class B17/1 3 cylinder 4-6-0 L.N.E.R. No. 2839 *"Rendelsham Hall"* is entering Thetford in August 1936. Large numbers of servicemen used to detrain at Thetford off this train to take the branch train to their camps, either on the Swaffham or Bury St. Edmunds lines.

No. 2839 was renamed *"Norwich City"* in 1938 — not surprisingly as the name should have been spelled "Rendlesham", and it had also been overlooked that Rendlesham Hall had become a high class nursing home for alcoholics and drug addicts.

▲ *Fig. 96* The mid-morning Thetford-Swaffham branch train nears Roudham Junction, hauled by Class E4 2-4-0 No. 62788 (pilot) and Class D1663 4-4-0 No. 62579 (train loco.).

This train was always double headed for operating purposes, connected with the trains provided for Thetford Grammar School pupils.

This branch was quoted in Dr. Beeching's report as the biggest money loser in East Anglia.

▼*Fig. 97* Class F3 2-4-2T L.N.E.R. No. 8066 on the Thetford-Bury St. Edmunds branch train crosses the old wooden trestle bridge near Barnham in August 1936.

The bridge survived the closure of passenger traffic on the branch on 8th June 1953, being replaced by a modern steel structure in 1954. The branch was closed to all traffic on 27th June 1960.

During the 1939-45 war, the camp at Barnham saw a great deal of railway activity, including nocturnal trains of poison gas, hauled by three J15 0-6-0s, two in front and one in the rear.

▲ *Fig. 98* This photo shows the Thetford-Bury St. Edmunds branch train at Barnham on an occasion when the train locomotive, Class F6 2-4-2T No. 67237 had failed. Class J15 0-6-0 No. 65420 (fitted with a spark arrester on account of the special traffic to the camp) which was shunting in the goods yard, was attached to provide the motive power for the train. Being a freight locomotive it was not fitted with the continuous brake. The braking was performed by No. 67237.

It must have been extremely rare for a freight locomotive not fitted with the continuous brake to carry a passenger train headcode, as in this photo.

◄ *Fig. 99* On 24th June 1960 Class J17 0-6-0 No. 65583 powers the last freight working through Thetford Bridge.

The very spacious station had originally been the terminus of the branch from Watton and a Thetford and Watton Railway rail chair survived in the goods yard till the line was taken up. The station was used to capacity at times for agricultural shows and military specials.

When Stratford was bombed in the 1939-45 war, it urgently needed a water column, which was taken from Thetford Bridge.

▲ *Fig. 100* At Swaffham the branch from Thetford joined the line from Dereham to Lynn. Middleton Towers, the station before Kings Lynn, had a very heavy sand traffic. As there was not a run round, the empties from Kings Lynn always had to be hauled by two locomotives.

On the day this photo was taken, the empties arrived at Middleton Towers behind Class J69/1 0-6-0Ts No. 68499 (pilot) and No. 68542 (train loco.).

These sand trains were powered by a great variety of combinations of locomotives.

▼ *Fig. 101* The Kings Lynn-Ely line, which today is part of British Rail's Inter-City network, was supplied with traffic off the Stoke Ferry branch at Denver Junction.

This branch is still open as far as Abbey for the British Sugar Corporation's traffic to and from its factory at Wissington. This is situated about two miles from Abbey, on what is now the only surviving section of the Wissington Railway. This was opened in 1906 to serve the fenland farms.

0-6-0T *"Wissington"* hauls a train working from the factory to the exchange sidings at Abbey.

▲ *Fig. 102* Another view of *"Wissington"* on a day when it was steaming badly. It is climbing up to the bridge over the river, banked in rear by a Manning Wardle 0-6-0ST No. 17. At one time this locomotive had belonged to the Bombay Port Trust.

▼ *Fig. 103* A Kings Lynn-March-Cambridge train crossing the River Ouse near Wiggenhall siding behind Class D16/3 4-4-0 No. 62572.

Many such wayside sidings were provided throughout the fens, when all the farm produce had to be brought to the railhead by horse and cart.

An Eastern Counties Railway seal was still being used daily at Emneth station on this branch, up to the closure of this line on 9th September 1968. The day's takings were put in a bag, duly sealed with the E.C.R. seal, and sent to the care of the Station Master at Wisbech.

Fig. 104 The River Nene was navigable by small ships up to Wisbech harbour. This was served by a Great Eastern Railway branch on its north side and a M. and G.N. branch on its south side. The tracks of the latter were still visible in 1950 as far as the very busy road bridge in the centre of the town.

Class J15 0-6-0 No. 65474 shunts the harbour on the Great Eastern branch.

Fig. 105 A roadside tramway was opened in August 1883 from Wisbech to Outwell, extended in the following year to Upwell.

Until 1952 it was worked by small specially designed tram locomotives, with cowcatchers and protected motion. They could be driven from either end.

Passenger traffic ceased on 2nd January 1928. The line remained open for freight till 25th May 1966.

This photo, taken in 1965, shows the train shunting at Outwell Basin. The locomotive is 204 h.p. Drewry class 04 No. D2201.

According to local tradition, the coach body, which had served as the station waiting room, had once been used as a saloon by Queen Victoria.

◀ *Fig. 106* A view of No. D2201, with its cowcatcher and enclosed motion, at Outwell Village.

In the foreground are the coal shutes used for loading barges which took the coal along the waterways to outlying farms. Even today, fenland roads are subject to subsidences.

Other instances of this rail — water co-operation were at Chatteris Dock, Two Mile Bottom (near Thetford) and at Burwell (at the end of the Burwell Tramway). The last two places had originally been developed for copralite traffic.

◀ *Fig. 107* In 1898 a freight line was constructed from Three Horse Shoes Junction, between March and Whittlesea, to Benwick. It was lightly laid over the fen and was always subject to subsidences.

Class J17 0-6-0 No. 65560 is at Benwick, where there was an extensive goods yard. Occasional passenger excursions had been run over the branch.

▲ *Fig. 108* Here Class J15 0-6-0 No. 65458 has arrived at Three Horse Shoes Junction from Benwick and is remarshalling its train. There were further marshalling yards at Whittlesea and Peterborough East, where the Great Eastern Railway shared the station with the London and North Western and Midland Railways.

Fig. 110 The March-St. Ives line became part of the G.N. and G.E. joint line in 1882, as did the branch ▶
from St. Ives to Huntingdon. The Great Eastern provided a local service between these two places. The
Midland Railway service from Kettering to Cambridge also had running powers over it.

In June 1932, Class D13 4-4-0 L.N.E.R. No. 8029 nears Cambridge on a March-Cambridge local train via
St. Ives.

The stock of the train is most interesting, being composed of half a suburban set, a six-wheeled van, a
clerestory bogie and a low-roofed non-clerestory bogie.

▲ *Fig. 109* Class J19 0-6-0 No. 64640 pauses at
Warboys, the intermediate station on the
Somersham-Ramsey East branch, which became
part of the Great Northern and Great Eastern
Joint line in 1882.

It was worked by the Great Eastern Railway,
who incidentally owned the branch from
Ramsey North to Holme on the Great Northern
main line. This was always leased to and
worked by the Great Northern Railway, the
line connecting the two stations at Ramsey
never having been built.

Fig. 111 Ely Cathedral dominates the fens and it can just be seen ▶
to the right of the platelayer's hut in this photo, where Class J17
0-6-0 No. 65576 is picking up trucks of sugar beet at Stretham.
This was the first station on the branch from Ely to St. Ives.

Passenger traffic ceased on the branch on 2nd February 1931
but a few excursions ran every summer to Yarmouth and
Hunstanton.

The last excursion over the whole branch from St. Ives ran in
1957. They continued to run from Sutton for a year or two
longer. The Sutton-Ely section remained open for freight till 5th
October 1964.

Fig. 113 Class J17 0-6-0 No. 65583 enters Haddenham (Cambs.); the very simple station building can be ▶
seen.

During the 1939-45 war, when London was blitzed and there was, in consequence, a heavy congestion of traffic at Cambridge, urgent supplies for East Anglia were sent to St. Ives over the Midland line from Kettering. Here the train was reversed and sent on to Ely.

▲ *Fig. 112* A picture showing Class J15 0-6-0 No. 65457, a rare visitor on the daily Ely-Sutton freight train. It is picking up trucks loaded with sugar beet at Wilburton, the next station to Stretham in October 1960.

Fig. 114 During the nineteen-fifties there was a daily freight train ▶ from Ely to Sutton. At the other end of the branch, Bluntisham, with a considerable timber traffic, was served by a daily train from St. Ives until 5th October 1964. Up to 1957 this train had served Earith Bridge when required, but as traffic fell off, the section from Bluntisham to Sutton was used for storing trucks, until it was completely closed on 6th October 1958.

This photo shows Class J17 0-6-0 No. 65532 approaching Earith Bridge.

A curiosity at this station was the down distant signal which retained a Coligny-Welch lamp, until the line was taken up.

Fig. 115 From Cambridge a branch ran to Fordham Junction and Mildenhall. In June 1932 Class B12 4-6-0 L.N.E.R No. 8526 is arriving at Mildenhall on a Sunday excursion which it had worked through from Liverpool Street.

This excursion was very well patronised, the short platforms at all the branch stations being packed with people who had come to meet their relatives off the train. The goods yards at every station were also completely full of trucks for outgoing agricultural produce and with incoming loads of stone for the fenland roads.

◄ *Fig. 117* Mildenhall had a large yard and was very spaciously laid out. Class J17 0-6-0 No. 65532 is leaving with a train of two loaded sugar beet trucks.

▲ *Fig. 118* Passenger traffic was withdrawn from the Mildenhall branch on 18th June 1962 and the freight service on 13th July 1964.

Many of the original signals on the branch remained till closure.

A Class J17 0-6-0 No. 65528 is passing the down branch Fordham Junction distant — a fine example with its tall post and Great Eastern finial. The signal lamp was situated half way down the post, separate from the signal arm, to give clear sighting at night.

Fig. 119 The Newmarket horse box traffic had been very important financially to the Great Eastern Railway. In this picture Class B1 4-6-0 No. 61205 is crossing the River Ouse near Ely on the morning train from Newmarket which connected with the North Country Continental express.

At the time this photo was taken, in March 1963, March was the only locomotive depot in East Anglia still using steam — and that chiefly on the joint line to the North. This morning working from Newmarket is believed to have been one of the very last to be steam hauled south of March.

Two seconds after this photo was taken, the snowstorm which can be seen approaching, completely blotted out everything.

As a measure of economy in the final days of the Ely-Newmarket passenger service, the signal box at Snailwell Junction was switched out in the afternoon. The d.m.us. which were by that time working the service had to run through to Chippenham Junction on the Newmarket-Bury St. Edmunds line. Here, in the middle of Newmarket Heath, the driver walked down the train and reversed it back to Newmarket. As the signal box at Newmarket was also closed in the afternoon, the train had to run on to Dullingham, as empty coaching stock, in order to return to Ely.

Fig. 120 Another branch which was owned by the Great Eastern Railway and yet never saw a Great Eastern train, was from Shelford Junction to Shepreth, where it made an end on junction with the Great Northern line from Kings Cross and Hitchin. This section was always leased to the Great Northern Railway.

After grouping in 1923, this route was used by the Royal Train on its way to Sandringham.

It was also used by race specials to Newmarket. This photo, taken in June 1931, shows Class C1 4-4-2 L.N.E.R. No. 4461 climbing up the bank from Newmarket to Dullingham with a first class Pullman special returning to Kings Cross.

Today the line from Newmarket to Cambridge, once important, can only be regarded as a minor branch.

An interesting survival at Dullingham in May 1977 was a pair of original Tommy Dodd signals controlling the cross over points.

▲ *Fig. 121* The cross country branch from Cambridge to Colchester has been mentioned before, a branch train being shown at Marks Tey (fig. 11).

In August 1934, Class J20 0-6-0 L.N.E.R. No. 8270 hauls a Cambridge train near Linton, composed largely of old Great Eastern Railway six-wheeled coaches.

The J20s were very powerful goods locomotives (their boilers were identical to those carried by the B12 4-6-0s) and — except for two — were not fitted with steam heating apparatus. They were rare on passenger trains.

They did their best work for years on the heavy coal trains from Whitemoor up to the London depots.

▲ *Fig. 122* Bartlow was the junction for Saffron Walden and Audley End. This line can be seen at the back of this photo in front of the signal box.

Class E4 2-4-0 No. 62784 is leaving on a Colchester train.

No. 62784 was withdrawn three days after this photo was taken, in May 1955.

Fig. 123 Class E4 2-4-0 No. 62788 is entering Haverhill on a ▶ Cambridge train in July 1956. The unusual water column will be noted.

The Station Master at Haverhill had a very good understanding of the local traffic requirements. He regretted the severance of all rail communication with Haverhill in March 1967 at the same time as a large overspill town from London was being built, and history would seem to have proved him right.

Fig. 124 The Colne Valley and Halstead Railway reached ▶ Haverhill on 10th May 1864, and it remained an independent company till the grouping in 1923, when it became part of the L.N.E.R.

Its trains connected at Haverhill with those of the Great Eastern Railway and, because of its shorter distance, reached Chappel ahead of the train that had left Haverhill before it.

It also had its own station at Haverhill South, where there was an engine shed. Haverhill South was used by the last night train from Chappel for several years after the grouping.

Class J15 0-6-0 No. 65573 is shunting at Haverhill South, which was not closed till 31st October 1966.

The remains of the station platforms can be seen beyond the brake van.

▲ *Fig. 125* A Colne Valley branch train enters White Colne, hauled by Class J15 0-6-0 No. 65470.

The small goods yard and booking office at this station were one side of a level crossing and the platform was the other. The body of a very old coach with square windows was used as a waiting room.

▼ *Fig. 126* Class E4 2-4-0 No. 62797 pulls out of Lavenham on a Long Melford-Bury St. Edmunds train.

Class J19 0-6-0 No. 64659 is in the siding. It has had to split its long train of empty coal wagons returning to the marshalling yard at Whitmoor. The rest of its train is in a siding beyond the bridge at the rear of the photo.

This branch saw heavy war traffic between 1939-45, remaining open all night.